Our poems
and no messin'

Poems from the classroom for assembly, RE and literacy work

compiled by Margaret Cooling

from a poetry competition

Scripture Union

THE STAPLEFORD CENTRE

ACt ASSOCIATION OF CHRISTIAN TEACHERS

© Scripture Union 1999
First published 1999

Scripture Union, 207–209 Queensway, Bletchley, Milton Keynes,
MK2 2EB

ISBN 1 85999 260 9

This book is published by Scripture Union in partnership with the
Stapleford Centre, Nottingham and the Association of Christian
Teachers.

British Library Cataloguing-in-Publication Data.
A catalogue record of this book is available from the British library.

Printed and bound in Great Britain by
Creative Print and Design (Wales), Ebbw Vale.

Illustrated by Kevin Wade

The Poetry Competition

In 1998 a poetry competition was announced as part of a partnership between Scripture Union, The Stapleford Centre and The Association of Christian Teachers who jointly sponsored the initiative.

Teachers and pupils were invited to send in poems under a number of categories. Most of these categories were Christian in content and included subjects such as Christmas, Easter, Jesus and the Holy Spirit. In addition, there were more general categories such as love, peace and friendship.

Over the year the poems arrived in small numbers, but the trickle became a flood after Poetry Day in October 1998. The entries came from all over the British Isles and also from Benin, Zambia, Pakistan and Denmark.

This book was compiled from over 1300 poems which were sent in by the end of October 1998. The poems were selected by Stewart Henderson (a well known poet), Margaret Cooling (a writer) and Elrose Hunter (Scripture Union's Commissioning Editor for children's books). Several criteria were borne in mind when making the selection.

1. Imagination freely expressed.
2. A certain uncluttered simplicity.
3. An attempt to grapple with a difficult, abstract idea in arresting language.
4. An accessible image.
5. A certain non-conformity in style or expression.
6. The creative use of language.
7. The ability to express an idea or feeling in a way that really captures its essence.
8. An unusual view of the world or the subject matter.

The choice was extremely difficult to make but all the poems selected fulfil one or more of the criteria.

As far as possible the children's layout and capitalisation, grammar etc. has been preserved. Occasionally minor alterations have been made.

Margaret Cooling has taught both primary and secondary pupils. For the last thirteen years she has been developing RE curriculum material for use in primary and secondary schools. She has written nearly thirty books for seven different publishers including the National Gallery and the BBC. Margaret also writes a regular magazine for primary schools called *Cracking RE*. To complement her writing Margaret works as a trainer, running in-service training across the country. She is based at the Stapleford Centre and is part of their curriculum development team.

Liverpool born performance poet, broadcaster and scriptwriter **Stewart Henderson** has had seven books of verse published. His most recent, *Limited Edition* immediately went into reprint when it appeared last summer, and his verse now appears in many leading poetry anthologies including the official Macmillan collection, *Read Me* for the National Year of Reading, a well as various GCSE set volumes. Recent trade reviews have begun to compare his work favourably with Manley Hopkins, Betjeman and even Eliot.

We warmly thank Stewart for giving us permission to use his poem 'Don't miss Christmas' which appears on page 56.

Contents

Poetry, RE, Assemblies and Literacy Teaching

The bell went and the pupils spilled out of the classroom. It was the end of an RE lesson, but the lesson was far from over. Pupils could still be heard discussing the RE topic all the way down the corridor. The discussion had been provoked by the teacher reading a child's poem. The class had then discussed the issue it raised: was God a God of love or a God of anger and judgement? After the discussion pupils had written their own poems. Poetry, particularly poetry written by children, has an important contribution to make in RE, assemblies and literacy teaching.

Why poetry written by children? One of the reasons for focusing on poetry written by children in this book is that the poems are at the right level and in the appropriate language for the classroom. They also encourage pupils to write their own poetry, as the example of other children shows what can be achieved.

Using poetry in Assemblies

Poems used for assemblies (collective worship) have to be of a particular type. Assemblies are short and there is little time for explanations. A poem therefore has to be understood on first reading, otherwise the assembly could be turned into an English lesson rather than have its rightful spiritual focus.

Some suggestions on how to use the poems in this book in planning Christian assemblies:

1. Select a poem which fits in with an assembly you have already planned. It can be used to illustrate an idea, express a feeling or be used as part of a time for prayer/reflection.

2. Design an assembly around a poem using the following guidelines:

   a) Read the poem through to yourself several times. Decide on its main theme.

   b) The theme of the poem should become the main focus of the assembly. All activities, stories, music and prayers should be chosen in order to explore the theme.

   c) Find ways of relating the theme to pupil experience. For example, if the poem is about friendship draw round one of the pupils on a piece of wallpaper (feet together) and display the shape on the wall. Ask pupils to suggest the qualities of a good friend and write their suggestions within the shape. This section on pupil experience can be used as an introduction to the assembly. When you have done this, decide how you are going to link pupil experience and the poem to the religious material – the link is not always obvious to pupils! Often a simple sentence is enough, but the link must be made.

   d) If the poem is a general one (not religious in content), decide if you want to use it alongside religious material. Such material could be a story from the Bible, a biography or a Christian belief or practice.

   e) Beware of assuming that pupils know the religious material which lies behind many of these poems. If the poem is based on a Bible story you will need to retell the story. You may need to explain a particular festival, belief or Christian practice which underpins a poem.

   f) Decide how you are going to get pupils to participate.

Are they going to read the poem or their own poems? Are they going to sing or take part in activities?

g) Finally, how are you going to include prayer and reflection in your assembly, and how are you going to create an atmosphere conducive to reflection? This may, for example, involve looking at the use of music, or using objects as a visual focus – such as a candle, an artefact or a cloth. Creating an atmosphere can include using prayers which involve many senses: touch, sight and sound as well as speech. It can also include silence.

When you have planned your assembly using these guidelines, run through this checklist very quickly:

a. Is the central theme clear?

b. Is there an appropriate balance between talking/activity and music, silence, reflection and prayer?

c. Can pupils participate in this assembly or are they remaining passive throughout it?

d. Has it got atmosphere?

Sample Assembly

You will need
- The poems *God decided to have some fun* and *Our Creator God* (pages 88 and 89)

- Party items such as whistles, hats, streamers etc.

- Balloons (already blown up with string attached)

- A large, safe, felt-tip pen

Introduction

Explain that this assembly is about having fun. Invite pupils to throw the streamers, blow whistles etc. Talk about things which are fun. Using pupil suggestions write up a list of fun things to do.

Core material

Read the story of Creation from a children's Bible. Explain that the story of Creation from the Bible shows God having fun. In the story God looked at Creation and said, 'That is good'.

Explain that Christians believe that God had fun when he made the world. He could have made it a dull and boring place; instead he filled it with colour and with beautiful creatures. Think what fun he must have had making the elephant's trunk, the camel's knees, butterfly's wings and the petals of a rose. Ask pupils to think of other animals and plants which would have been fun to make.

Read the poems *God decided to have some fun* and *Our Creator God* and show a picture of a duck-billed platypus (optional).

Prayer/reflection

Show the balloons. On each balloon the teacher can write some of the things which pupils suggested God had fun making. On the last balloon write the word 'people'. Invite several pupils to come to the front. Each one can say a one-line prayer:

'Thank you God for making the (say what is on the balloon).'

Once the prayer is said the balloon is patted upwards. (Keep hold of the string; this stops it hitting lights etc.) When the balloon descends it can be displayed.

Music to enter and leave
Some suitable party music to create an atmosphere of excitement.

Poetry and RE

Poems can also be part of RE. They can be used in a number of ways.

1. To stimulate pupils' thinking.

2. To highlight an issue.

3. To show how people in faith stories express their feelings on a particular subject.

4. To stimulate pupils to express their own ideas through poetry.

5. To show how Christians relate religious material to everyday life.

Poems for RE need to be of a particular type. There is more time in an RE lesson to explore what a poet is saying so the poems do not have to be instantly understood. You can read a poem more than once and there is time to discuss an allusion or metaphor. However, RE should not become an English lesson.

When designing an RE lesson using poetry the following questions should be asked:

a. What is the theme/content/subject I want to teach? What are my aims and objectives for this lesson? (Teachers should refer to their RE Syllabus and scheme of work for this.) Once you have decided this, select a poem which will help you achieve it.

b. Does the poem I have chosen help to provoke conversation amongst the pupils so that they will discuss the subject in hand? If the poem closes down conversation rather than stimulates it, you may need to choose another poem or activity to stimulate conversation. You could decide to use the original poem you selected in a different way; for example, it could be used to finish the lesson as a closing thought.

c. Does the lesson I have planned allow pupils time to reflect on the issue or is it all activity based? Where can I plan in time for reflection?

d. Can pupils see the relevance of the material to their own experience? How can I help them do this?

Sample RE lesson

Aim

To understand that Christians believe a person should stand up for their faith. To explore the idea that not all laws are good and that Christians believe that God's laws are higher than human laws.

Introduction

Tell the story of Daniel either from a children's Bible or, if possible, use the version called *'Dinner in the Lions' Den'* from

14

Angels Angels All Around by Bob Hartman published by Lion (suitable for juniors).

Exploring the story
Conversation/discussion points
What got Daniel into trouble? Was he doing something that we would normally say was wrong? Daniel broke the law. Is it sometimes right to break a law? Ask pupils to make up a bad law that they would think it would be right to disobey. Explain that Christians believe that God's laws come first so that if leaders make up a law that tells people to do something wrong, then Christians believe that law can be broken. Note: this should not be misunderstood and interpreted as the right to break any inconvenient law.

Read the poem *Daniel* (page 25). Has the poem captured what is important about the story? How has it done that? In what way was the lions' den *'a friendship only zone'?* Was the friendship only between Daniel and the lions? Was Daniel alone in the lion pit?

Activity
Rearrange the poem for a narrator and two voices: Daniel and a lion. Colour the parts so that people know when to speak. Present the poem as other people mime it. Retell the story of Daniel in your own words, emphasising the parts where a bad law is made and Daniel stands up for what he believes. How would the story have been different if either Daniel or Darius had behaved differently? Write an alternative ending.

Think about it

Today people are not thrown to lions but standing up for what you believe can still be very difficult. It often means behaving differently to everyone else – which is hard to do. The idea of opposing bad laws can be followed up using modern biography such as Desmond Tutu or Martin Luther King.

Poetry and Literacy Teaching

A much wider range of poems can be used in literacy teaching, as the poem is the main focus and it *is* an English lesson. More time can be given to matters such as structure, language and form. There is a poetry strand in the *National Literacy Strategy* and in the Welsh, Northern Irish and Scottish literacy/English documents. Some of the ways in which poetry can be used in literacy teaching are listed below. Note: most of the examples given are included in the English *National Literacy Strategy*, but they are also part of general literacy/language work and can be used in any setting.

Reading poems

Pupils can discuss how the message, atmosphere and meaning of a poem is conveyed. Give pupils several poems from the book linked by a theme. Ask pupils to identify and discuss the theme which links them. Class anthologies of favourite poems from the book can be created, but pupils should justify their choices. Poems can be learnt by heart, or they can be prepared for reading aloud, taking account of meaning, rhythm and punctuation. Attention should be paid to expression, tone, volume and the use of different voices. Mime, dance or actions can be added to some poems.

Writing poetry

Sound poems (pages 80 and 92), cinquains (page 66), alliterative poems (page 68), shape poems (page 29), acrostics (page 25) and metaphor poems (page 32) can all be created using the poems in this book as models.

Rhyme, Rhythm

Using a poem such as *Lord what can you make of me?* (page 32), pupils can work out a poem's rhyme pattern and use it as a model for their own poems (the subject can be different). They can clap rhythms and use percussion instruments to highlight the rhythm of a poem. Using the poem *The World* (page 65) and *Harvest* (page 34), pupils can compare and contrast poems which rhyme and poems which do not.

Humour

Poems such as *Our Creator God* (page 88) and *Daniel* (page 25) can be used as examples of humorous poems. Pupils can explore how the poet has made them funny. Where does the humour lie? Does it help convey the message of the poem?

Poets

Two poems by the same person (pages 62 and 34 and pages 92 and 95) can be compared and their style can be described. A child's poem can also be read alongside a poem by a well known poet on the same subject. For example, read the poem by Stewart Henderson (page 56) alongside some of the Christmas poems by pupils (page 58–60). Explore the way ideas about Christmas are expressed by the different poets.

Sample Literacy Activity

Whole class shared text work

Photocopy the poem *'Lord What Can You Make of Me?'* on to an acetate and put it up on an overhead projector. Read it through several times with the pupils. With younger pupils identify the rhyme and the pattern of the poem. With older pupils identify the metaphors and what the metaphors are saying. For example: *'I'm only a twig, make me a log'*. The metaphors describe the person who is praying. Discuss what these metaphors are saying in the context of prayer. (They are asking God to help them to reach their full potential). Pupils can suggest new lines using the same pattern.

Whole class word level work

Take one of the rhymes and ask pupils to find other words that will rhyme with it (twig, big, etc.). Repeat this with other rhymes and create rhyme lists. Together look at the structure of the lines and create a language template using the same punctuation and word pattern: *I'm only a ..., make me a ... .*

Group and independent work

Using the template, younger pupils can create their own new lines. With older pupils, these can be illustrated to demonstrate how metaphors create pictures in people's minds. This can be extended to creating a class poem. Older pupils can make it rhyme, using the rhyme lists created earlier.

The plenary

Review the work pupils have done. Pupils can share their metaphors/new lines with the whole class.

Further resources

Poetry and Writing Toolkit, Story and Drama Toolkit: creative ideas for using the Bible in the classroom Margaret Cooling (Bible Society 1996).

Literacy/RE packs which include poetry:
Pack 1 *Lost and Found (5–7)* Narrative (Fiction)
Pack 2 *Lost and Found (5–7)* Non-Fiction
Pack 3 *Heroes and Heroines (7–11)* Narrative (Fiction)
Pack 4 *Heroes and Heroines (7–11)* Non-Fiction

All available from the Stapleford Centre (Wesley Place, Stapleford, Nottingham NG9 8PD).

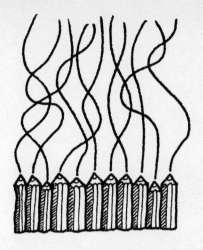

Bible People

Bathsheba's Lament

My brave old man
died in the war.
All I can see
is his bloodstained shirt
in my hands.
Lying there in your grave,
looking up at me,
I see you through my tears
just like before.
Just sadness lies between us.
Your flashing sword is in front of me,
your face is in the fire,
your eyes are blazing red.
I see you in your shield,
your sword as well.
Where are you? In the ground
or up in the sky?
As strong as a hurricane
you are in my eyes,
as you march in front of the line.
Brave as can be,
brave as a bear.
When will I see you again?
Your armour is shining in the light.
I think you are there
but I know you're not.
Killed with a spear
as you fought there.

I cry in sorrow as I see you.
The battle is fierce and still going on,
for you are gone
and we are losing.
You lie in heaven.
You lie in the ground.
Where have you gone?
Where is your love?
I am all alone,
my heart is heavy
with sorrow
and broken love.
Where are you?
In the sky or in the ground?
Where are you?
Between our love I see you.
But have you gone
… or me?

Jasmin Stevens (8)
Charlton Kings Junior School, Cheltenham, Glos

Zacchaeus

When the crowd looked at Zacchaeus

    they saw...

a man who was a thief
a man who was mean
a man who didn't care
a greedy man

BUT,

When Jesus looked at Zacchaeus

    he saw...

a man who could be friendly
a man who could care
a man who could change
a different man.

Fiona Mulley (8)
Great Barton School, Bury St. Edmunds, Suffolk

Daniel

Daniel prayed to God and then
he ended up inside the den.
The lion said, "What are you doing here?"
Daniel said, "I have no fear.
I prayed too much, but God is near."
The lion said, "You are too thin
I need more meat upon the bone."
This partnership made the lion's den a
Friendship only zone.

Rachael Evans (8)
Hall School, Wimbledon, London

FLOOD!

Flood
Land
Olive leaf
Overjoyed
Dove

Rachael Murray (9)
Ince C of E Primary School, Wigan

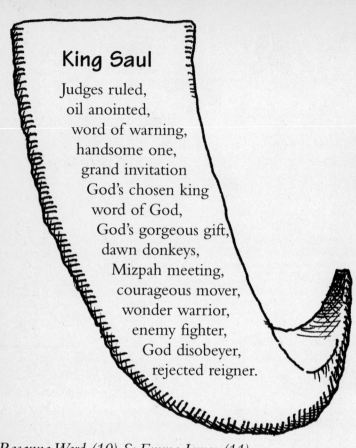

King Saul

Judges ruled,
oil anointed,
word of warning,
handsome one,
grand invitation
God's chosen king
word of God,
God's gorgeous gift,
dawn donkeys,
Mizpah meeting,
courageous mover,
wonder warrior,
enemy fighter,
God disobeyer,
rejected reigner.

Rosanna Ward (10) & Emma James (11)
St Ives School, Haslemere, Surrey

Noah and his animals

Time: 7.45
Place: Ark
Person: Noah
Weather: Absolutely tipping it down

What shall I do?
I have ...
kangaroos, tortoises,
lizards, porpoises,
sheep, drakes,
cows, snakes,
fish, dogs,
sharks, frogs,
giraffes, cats,
fleas, bats,
deer, mice,
wolves, lice,
lions, monkeys,
tigers, donkeys,
What a hullabaloo!
The donkeys are braying,
the horses are neighing,
the fleas are biting,
the cats are fighting,
the monkeys are howling,
The dogs are growling.
O what shall I do?
The shark's eaten the fish.
What a good dish.
Cats eating mice
and lice.
JUST another 39 days to go!

Jocelyn King (9)
St Mellons C/W Primary, Llanrumney,
Cardiff

David

David was a roaring fire
blazing in the grate.
He was as bright as a bolt of
lightning and just as fast.
Saul tried to put him out many a time.
But the boy of a lightning bolt
dodged the deadly spear.

Philip McAdam (11)
Sakeji School, Zambia

Goliath

If he were a colour he would be red.
If he were a plant he would be a massive oak.
If he were a fruit he would be a lemon.
If he were weather he would be a thunderstorm.
If he were an animal he would be an elephant.

Aden Van Langenberg (7)
Parakou Christian School, Benin

Noah's Ark

Start

drops, rainbow round,

boat rocks, rain

land ashore, little

Animals noisy,

bird brings

hope, happy Noah, animals

goes right through, bright sun.

two by two, little bird, faithful flew,

Kylie Pursglove (9)
St. Thomas' CE (A) Primary, Kidsgrove,
Stoke-on-Trent, Staffs

Zaccheus

If he was a tree he would be a thornbush.
If he was a flower he would be a thistle.
If he was a vegetable he would be an onion.
If he was a colour he would be purple.
If he was weather he would be a cloudy day.

Mark Corke (10)
St. Thomas' CE (A) Primary, Kidsgrove,
Stoke-on-Trent, Staffs

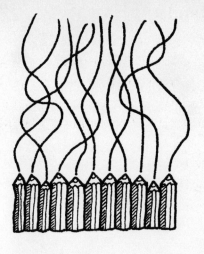

Prayer

Lord, what can you make of me?

I am only a twig. Make me a log.
I am only a piglet. Make me a hog.
I am only a letter. Make me a word.
I am only an egg. Make me a bird.
I am only a leaf. Make me a tree.
I am only a drop. Make me a sea.

Emily Drew (10)
Danetree School, West Ewell, Surrey

Ian's Blessing

May God keep you safe.
May the wind point you in the right direction.

May you see all the world and its creatures,
and may the flowers open up for you.

May the sun shine on you every day,
until the next time we meet.

May God bless you in every way.

Ian Edmondson (9)
Crosscrake CE School, Stainton, Kendal, Cumbria

The bad thing

Sad, depressed face, cut, grazed face.
I can't bear it any longer
I can't bear it any longer
I can't bear it any more.
I just wish people would forget it
I just wish people would forget it
I just wish people would forget it
I just wish people would forget it now.
Dusty, misty, horrible place.
Dirty, littery, polluted place.
I can't bear it any longer
I can't bear it any more
I just wish people would forget it now
I just wish people would forget it now
I just want to go home
Cause
I want
I want
I want
I want
I want
to go home.

Kelly Frewin (10)
Burton CE Primary School, Christchurch, Dorset.

A prayer

written for the School's Harvest Festival, October 1997

Heavenly Father,
Can you hear me?
Are you listening?
I was wondering
if you'd have time
just to listen to
what I have to say –
Do you?

I just wanted
to thank you, Lord,
for all you've given me,
For the beautiful world
for me to enjoy.

I was hoping, God,
You might be able to help me
when I ask:
will you lay a blessing
on the people less fortunate than me?

It might help me
feel less guilty
standing here in my rich world,
but still in harmony with you,
my Heavenly Father.

Amen

Katherine Davidson (10)
St James' CE Primary School, Weybridge, Surrey

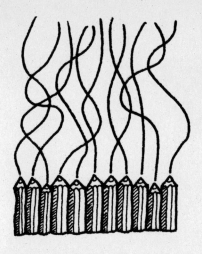

Easter

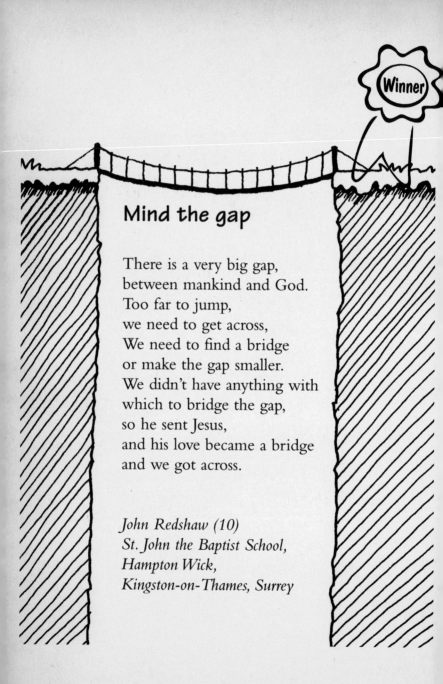

Mind the gap

There is a very big gap,
between mankind and God.
Too far to jump,
we need to get across,
We need to find a bridge
or make the gap smaller.
We didn't have anything with
which to bridge the gap,
so he sent Jesus,
and his love became a bridge
and we got across.

John Redshaw (10)
St. John the Baptist School,
Hampton Wick,
Kingston-on-Thames, Surrey

The day he died

As I saw the man in pain,
I saw the whippers again and again.
The blood ran down and he felt sore,
then the soldiers whipped some more.
As I saw the king walk slowly past.

The special king,

the first,

the last.

A person said, how much do you love
us?
He stretched out his arms and then
he died for us.

Sarah Lyttleton (11)
Holden Lane Primary School, Stoke-on-Trent, Staffs

The man born to be king

Trudging up the steep
hill in agony.
Collapsing in pain,
sweat seeping out,
transforming to blood.

Soon he is up
ready to be killed,
being stripped and
hung up high.

Watchers laughing,
disciples stepping back
scared and afraid.
Women upset, feeling
his pain.
Mary is there tearful
and sad.
People kneel and pray,
for the man born to be king forever.

Amy Cannell (11)
Holy Trinity Junior School, Guildford, Surrey

At the cross

The bitter tears shed by the sorrowful
mother, lingered in my mouth.

There is fear ascending in the bleak air, as
it drifts up my nose.

The rusty, bent nails holding him prisoner
with their evil grasp.
I can still picture it in my mind.

The pain and sorrow felt by Jesus' disciples
and his many friends reaches me
as I touched the rough, blood-stained wood
Jesus died on.

The sound of Jesus being tormented,
his heart wilting and crying out loud.
It rings and echoes in my ears.

And in my heart I feel a great loss,
when Jesus died on the cross
for all our wrongdoings.

Robert Boswell (10)
Mudeford Junior School, Christchurch, Dorset

At the cross

I can taste the terrible pain
and agony of the death.

I can smell the fear and
pain of Jesus' friends.

I can see the mother of Jesus
and her salty tears.

I can touch the large unforgiving
rough cross.

I can hear the distressed
and heartbroken mother and
the laughter of the soldiers.

And in my heart I feel
tearful but most of all sorrowful.

Taryn Harper (10)
Mudeford Junior School, Christchurch, Dorset

42

At the cross

The Romans' sweat drips from
their faces to
hit the ground and
disappear into the soil.
There is a scent sap from
the freshly cut tree.
Thin spikes dig into his skin.
There is blood
running down the wood from his
back.
A dice is
rolling over
the uneven ground.

Pain is all I feel.

Dean Prodomo (10)
Mudeford Junior School, Christchurch, Dorset

The sadness I feel

Time: 10:15am
Person: Mary
Place: Standing below the cross
Weather: Cold and dark

He hangs on the cross
silent and still.
Is he dead?
My only son!
God's son!
Nails in his hands
glinting nastily like demon crystals.
A thorny crown on his head,
soldiers mocking.
Why Jesus?
Why him?
Suddenly Jesus cries
"Forgive them, Father,
for they know not
what they do!"
Suddenly tears well up
like a waterfall behind a dam.
Suddenly the dam breaks.
I sob out loud!
"Jesus!" I cry.
Jesus turns to
the disciple he loves

and says "She is your mother".
He turns to me and says
"He is your son".
I sob more.
He closes his eyes.
He is dead!
And all our hopes die with him.
Nobody could ever experience
the sadness I feel.

Sophie Reed (10)
St. Mellons C/W Primary, Llanrumney, Cardiff

The crucifixion

Painfully I carry my cross
up the big hill,
whipped all the way.
I lie down on the cross.
I am nailed down with huge nails.
The cross is knocked into the ground.
My family stands weeping.
Goodbye my friends,
I will be back.

Joshua Pearce (10)
St. John the Baptist School, Hampton Wick,
Kingston-on-Thames, Surrey

Jesus is risen

12.00pm and the stars are shining
brightly like 100 candles.
In an upper room with a nice calm
soft breeze coming through the window,
Thomas wanted to see Jesus in person.
Jesus appeared,
Thomas believed.
He knelt before Jesus.
"My king" he said.

Daniel Watts (9)
Rudgwick County Primary School, Horsham,
West Sussex

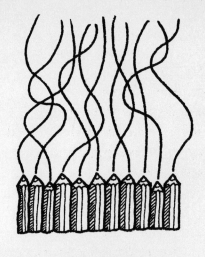

General

Friendship

When we were younger, much
   younger,
we used to finish each other's
   sentences,
anticipating heartfelt thoughts.
We used to point rudely and stare, wide-eyed.
We used to burst into unprovoked giggles
over something small, something unimportant.
We used to talk about nothing in particular, for
   hours.

Times have changed, so have we.
Now we each have someone else special to do
   all that with.
A new friend, the same qualities but not
   identical.

Alice Bennett (10)
Steeple Morden CE Primary School, Royston, Herts

Peace

I am the peace that kills the wars,
I am the peace that closes doors,
I am the peace that slithers in the sea,
I am the peace as calm as can be,
I am the peace that stands in the silence,
I am the peace that stops all violence.

This is the peace that brings joy and laughter.
This is the peace that will live ever after.

Zohra Bandali (10)
Broadwater Primary School, Tooting, London

Peace is...

reading in my bedroom and listening to music

having hot milk or cocoa at night

painting pictures of landscapes

animals wandering in the peaceful countryside

birdsong in the morning outside

freedom of speech

silently sleeping in my nice warm bed.

Peace, help me relax.

Steven Livingstone (11)
Eaton Park Primary School,
Bucknall, Stoke-on-Trent, Staffs

Love

If love was something in the world it would be
   the air.
If love were weather it would be sunshine.
If love were a plant it would be grass.
If love were a colour it would be red.
If love were a flower it would be a rose.
If love were a bird it would be a robin.
If love were an animal it would be a rabbit.

Rhiannon Searle (9)
Nodehill Middle School, Newport, IOW

Feelings

When I am angry
I feel as red
as a blazing fire.

When I am bored
I feel as blue
as the salty sea.

When I am happy
I feel as yellow as the sun
in the sky.

When I am glad
I feel as green
as the grass on the ground.

Peter Matthews (7)
St James' Lanehead CE Primary School, Burnley,
Lancs

My Will

To my grandad I leave my hope,
for his wife is gone forever.

To my brother I leave my voice,
for he does not do too well in choir.

And lastly I leave my love to my mum and dad,
for those are the ones I really love.

Rebecca Farndale (10)
Steeple Morden CE Primary School, Royston, Herts

Love

Love

is

a man

dying

for God.

Alexander Draper (8)
Richard Hill CE (Aided) Primary School, Thurcaston,
Leicester

Friends

Friends are like fire,
spreading across vast areas
and reaching out for everything in its path.
But when something new and different comes
along – like water,
it can all extinguish with one blast
so your friendship is left as history, as ash.
But sometimes there's a spark.
If you save that spark,
you can light it again.
Your friendship can start again,
slowly return to what you had.

Daisy Shirley-Beavan (10)
Steeple Morden CE Primary School, Royston, Herts

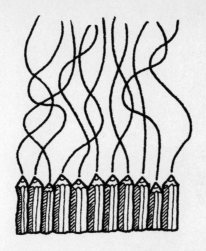

Christmas

Don't miss Christmas

Don't miss Christmas
Whilst yearning for the snow
and planning deft manoeuvres
towards the mistletoe
The turkey turning golden
as the sprouts begin to steam
the pudding glazed with brandy
and smashed on double cream

Don't miss Christmas
as mince pies singe your tongue
and you scowl behind your port
at decorations badly hung
where strange relations gather
like a loud, annoying swarm
when the fat logs spit and crackle,
but the homeless can't keep warm

Don't miss Christmas
beware the muddled shelves
displaying Game Boy reindeer
destroying Santa's elves
whilst Mortal Kombat shepherds
chase dragons through the town
the three kings never showed
their helicopter's been shot down

Don't miss Christmas
absorb the silent night
and watch the mucous Saviour
arrive from heaven's height
as in the holy darkness
a virgin strains, then cries,
God's helpless, breathing icon
appears with Mary's sighs

Don't miss Christmas –
the magic of it all
our brittle, gift-wrapped anthem
sleeps in a cattle stall
as the poor and lost and starving
weakly start to sing
it seems only desperate subjects
recognise their King.

Stewart Henderson

Christmas

The love and the light that
this child has brought us.

Powerless King Herod can do
nothing against him.
Everyone rejoices in Jesus
the
saviour.
But diminished King Herod
wears a
cold crown on his
head.

Alistair Sim (11)
Steeple Morden CE Primary School, Royston, Herts

Glorious God

Glorious God of all hopes.

Of candles and Christmas and birth.

Despair not, for God is with you.

Jessica Beales (7)
Aldrington CE Primary School, Hove, East Sussex

Why?

Why in a manger?
Why on a cross?
Why did he suffer
for sinful us?

Why not a palace?
Why not a bed?
Why not a crown
upon his head?

He slept in a manger,
he had to die,
because he loved us.
That's why!

Naomi Nicolson (11)
Firth Primary School, Finstown, Orkney

Baby Jesus

I saw Jesus in the manger,
I heard him slightly sighing
and I smelt the fresh hay.
Jesus had the taste of a King.
I felt his soft peach face.
After I had seen him
I went home rejoicing,
singing and spreading the good news
to everyone I saw!

Rhona Park (9)
Sakeji School, Zambia

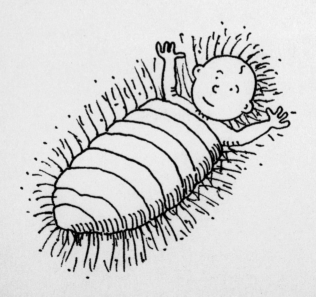

Creation

Creation

Monday
There was a mighty bang!
As the ball bounced off the ceiling
and into the basin.
The new electric lights
were then switched on.
They glittered like the sun.

Tuesday
The morning was cold and dewy,
Unfortunately
the ball had been left outside
the previous night.
Water droplets had gathered on the ball
and it was enveloped in mist.

Wednesday
Green mould began to appear
on the damp ball
For it had not been cleaned.
New kinds of blue
and brown moulds
began to grow amongst the green
fluff.

Thursday
Lights were installed.
The bright lamp
was lit during the day
and a torch
was used at night.
The ceiling was full of holes
which let only specks of light
into the dark room
and gave a starry
appearance.

Friday
The ball was left out in the garden
again.
It had things living in it
and winged things
hovered above it
buzzing furiously.
Singled celled micro-organisms
began to grow in the water droplets.

Saturday
Then people appeared around the ball.
Men and women
and it became their own.
They had control of the creatures
and the 'land'
and the 'seas'.

Sunday

On Sunday the ball was lost.
The dog probably took it
to a damp compost heap
at the bottom of the garden
and buried it
with the other nine missing playthings;
the huge yellow football,
the small red ping-pong ball,
the orange ball from last Christmas,
the red tennis ball,
the large swirly rugby ball,
a turquoise ball with rings of scum around it,
a small green ball,
the blue ball,
and
the tiny marble.
Meanwhile, he rested
For he had made the Earth.

Katherine Davidson (11)
St. James' CE Primary School, Weybridge, Surrey

The world

Plants on the land,
fish in the sea,
birds in the sky,
forests full of trees.

Houses, shops, schools,
cars, buses, trains,
mountains, hills, fields,
bikes, boats and planes.

Many, many countries,
different people living there,
this great world is where I live.
It needs a lot of care.

Katy Sealy (8)
Bawdsey CE VC Primary School, Woodbridge, Suffolk

Creation cinquains

First:
From emptiness
night and day,
'Let there be light!'
shining.   **Second:**
God separating,
sea from sea,
creating the spacious, heavenly
sky.   **Third:**
rocky land,
watery widespread oceans,
trees and plants growing,
verdant.   **Fourth:**
glorious lights,
seasons, days, years,
stars gleaming every night,
sparkling.

Junior Class (9/10)
Crosscrake CE School, Stainton, Kendal, Cumbria

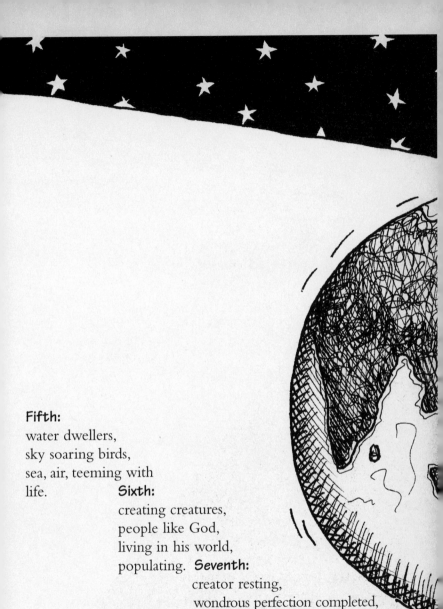

Fifth:
water dwellers,
sky soaring birds,
sea, air, teeming with
life.　　**Sixth:**
　　creating creatures,
　　people like God,
　　living in his world,
　　populating.　**Seventh:**
　　　creator resting,
　　　wondrous perfection completed,
　　　God blessed the day,
　　　Sunday.

67

God

God made gigantic green trees.

God made silent spreading trees.

God made fragrant flowers.

God made marvellous me!

God made the growing grass

and the energetic earth.

God made everything.

Hugh Hannah (9)
Eastbank Primary School, Shettleston, Glasgow

Sun and moon

I used to see the sun just as the sun.
Yellow, lifeless, just a circle in the sky.
But one day you opened my eyes.
It was like a diamond in the sky,
a yellow balloon,
an egg yolk.
Thank you for opening my eyes.

I used to see the moon just as the moon.
Lifeless, just a circle in the sky.
But one day you opened my eyes.
It was like a 10 pence on a blue carpet,
a silver light and a white button on a blue coat.
Thank you God for opening my eyes.

Claire Moffat (9)
Newlaithes Junior School, Carlisle, Cumbria

Creation

I saw a field full of corn,
I saw a lamb being born,
I saw two trees swaying in the breeze.
God created all of these.

I saw some cheetahs feeding,
I heard the church bells ringing,
I saw people praying on their knees.
God created all of these.

I saw some ants marching home,
I saw an old lady all alone,
I saw a child saying, 'Please'.
God created all of these.

Lucy Keyzor (9)
Nodehill Middle School, Newport, IOW

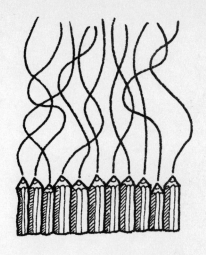

God, Jesus

and

Holy Spirit

God

God is good, giving and great

Opens up to others and

Does delightful things

Leonie Conroy (9)
Eastbank Primary School, Shettleston, Glasgow

God

God is
a big tree
a small bee
a king of kings
a knight of knights
a light so bright
than any I've seen.

Anthony Braines (10)
Richard Hill CE (Aided) Primary School, Thurcaston,
Leicester

Jesus is in everything

If Jesus was a colour, he would
be a fresh spring green.
If Jesus was a tree he would be
a tall silky silver birch.
If Jesus was a food he would be
a dark rich chocolate cake.
If Jesus was a drink he would be
clear sparkling water.
If Jesus was a flower he would
be a baby pink carnation.
But all in all what I'm trying to say
is Jesus is wonderful in every way.

Natalie Holden (10)
Rygards School, Hellerup, Denmark

Spring

Spring is here, winter's kingdom crashes,
as its empire fades away.
The time of callousness turns to ashes,
the days of winter are spent.

>Warmth is here, winter crashes,
>the Holy Spirit's in the air.

Winter strengthens into summer,
the spring maiden nurses nature back to health.
The medicine is working; the season rises from
  slumber.
Let life return to Earth again.

>Warmth is here, winter crashes,
>the Holy Spirit's in the air.

The darkness fades, the tomb is opened,
on the earth children play.
The gates of Heaven are reopened,

God has created the world again.

Warmth is here, winter crashes,
the Holy Spirit's in the air.

Look around you, see Earth's wonders,
that sprang from His blood.
He was sacrificed as storms thundered,
he rose again, God the Son.

Warmth is here, winter crashes,
the Holy Spirit's in the air.

Jonathan Aitken (11)
St Mellons C/W Primary School, Llanrumney, Cardiff

The Poem of Mary

Time: 1.00pm
Person: Mary
Place: House in Nazareth
Weather: Hot sunny day

Here I am looking out of my window.
I am watching my strong hardworking
    son helping his father.
My husband is a carpenter and a very
    good one too.
My son is sawing away at that mighty
    wood with those hands.
I know that one day those sturdy
    muscular hands will be fighting for

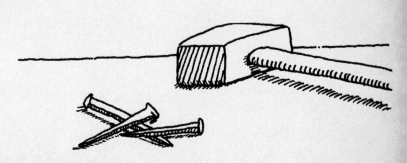

peace throughout the world.
They will be full of love and comfort.
I can tell that your feet are aching.
I think that you are a tough mighty
  warrior.
You will give the people of this
  world a good normal life.
Those feet will someday be
  worshipped.
They will ache from telling the
  people of this world about God.
Those nails that you're hammering in
  that piece of wood,
    will some day and somehow be in you.

Faye Bezant (10)
St. Mellons C/W Primary School, Llanrumney, Cardiff

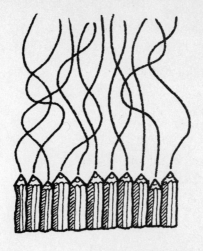

The Bible

Winner

The story of the Good Samaritan

Crinchity crunch crinchity crunch crinchity crunch
BANG WALLOP help! **SMACK** ow! **SMASH**
Where's the money? **KICK** stop it!
Rush rush rush rush rush rush.
GONE

Crinchity crunch crinchity crunch crinchity crunch
STOP
Oooh, oh no, poor man,
In a hurry hurry hurry hurry
GONE

Tick tock tick tock tick tock
Tweet tweet
Tick tock tick tock tick tock
Slither slither
Tick tock tick tock tick tock

Crinchity crunch crinchity crunch crinchity crunch
STOP
Oooh, oh no, poor man,
It's dangerous, dangerous, dangerous, dangerous,
GONE

Tick tock tick tock tick tock
Sizzle sizzle
Tick tock tick tock tick tock

Clip clop clip clop clip clop
STOP
Oooh, oh no, poor man,
Crunch
Smooth soothe
Drip drip rip rip
Calm balm
Drip drip rip rip
Cool, aaaah
Shade, aaaah
Alley oop!
Crintchity crunch
Clip clop
Crintchity crunch
Clip clop
STOP

Aaaaaaah
Tick tock tick tock tick tock
Hoot hoot
Tick tock tick tock tick tock
Aa-ooooo
Tick tock tick tock tick tock
Zzzzzzz Zzzzzzz
Tick tock tick tock tick tock

Woooooooo
Tick tock tick tock tick tock
Cock a doodle doo!

Chingle chingle
See you soon!
Clip clop clip clop clip clop clip clop clip clop clip clop

Class 3M (8)
Highcliffe Junior School (GM), Christchurch, Dorset

The Bible

The Bible is a special book,
not one, but sixty-six.
Different people wrote it,
it is a special mix
of history and poetry,
people good and bad,
things to make you happy,
and things to make you sad.
The Bible is God's Book,
it tells of Jesus too.
parts of it are very old
but it is always new.

Junior Class (9)
The Abbey School, Farnham, Surrey

The storm

Giant waves splashed loudly
terrified friends panicked madly
crashing rain drenched heavily
rowing boat swung fiercely
strong storm roared powerfully
blinding lightning flashed brightly
scared disciples complained bitterly
calm Jesus slept deeply
powerful Jesus spoke commandingly
rough storm stopped immediately.

Naomi Locke (9)
St. Thomas' CE (A) Primary School, Kidsgrove,
Stoke-on-Trent, Staffs

Bible

I get my favourite book out and look at the front
cover.
'Bible'

written in gold letters across the
front, and entwined in the letters,
creepers with big blooming flowers
of different colours, and underneath
a picture of a man, I think it must be

Jesus.

Surrounding him are animals, children,
plants, adults, sunshine and snow.
I gaze at the picture for some time
before I put the

Bible

back in its place, its special place
at the top of the bookcase and go
upstairs to bed.

Claire Willoughby (10)
Thriplow CE (Aided) Primary School, Royston, Herts

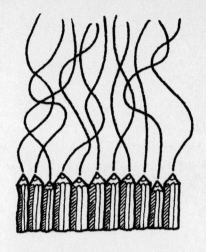

Infant
entries

Jesus and us

Jesus and God
love me and I love them.
Together we go through the world
just so.

Nicky Jackson (7)
Eaton Park Primary School, Bucknall, Stoke-on-Trent,
Staffs

God is ...

God is as big as a house
God is as happy as yes
God is as strong as a whole school
God is as big as the whole world
God is mightier than a tornado
God is as old as a great grandad
God makes the sun shine on me
God is sad when he sees people starve
Thank you God for food.

Lyam Brabson (6)
Frederick Harrison Infant School, Stapleford,
Nottingham

Thank you God for...

red butterflies that fly,
green grass that wobbles,
purple flowers that smell,
black spiders that tickle,
Yellow giraffes that walk,
Orange tigers that bite,
And me.

Jade Poole (5)
Frederick Harrison Infant School, Stapleford,
Nottingham

Harvest

Great grapes
big broccoli
bright bananas
purple plums
curly cabbage
Oh for a lovely orange.

Kia Tasbihgou (6)
Homewood School, St Albans, Herts

Our Creator God

God woke up one morning
and said to himself
"It would be nice
to have a duck-billed platypus."
So he thought he would colour it
a chocolate brown.

Then he said that it would have
a tail like a beaver
and he made its body
like a beaver too.
He thought he would put
a duck's beak on it.

Then he decided
to make it lay eggs,
not to have a live baby,
and its character
is going to be funny!

God looked at his design
and thought it was
extremely ridiculous!

Eleanor Ineson (7)
St Thomas' CE School, Kendal Green, Kendal,
Cumbria.

God made the world

God made the world
so we could be free.
Thank you God for
making me.

Jamie Charlton (6)
Whitley Chapel CE (A) First School, Steel, Hexham,
Northumberland

God decided to have some fun

God decided to have some fun.
He created the sun
plants and trees
stars and moon
animals, flowers and
the monsoon.
Thank you God for
this wonderful world.

William Crozier (5)
Whitley Chapel CE (A) First School, Steel, Hexham,
Northumberland

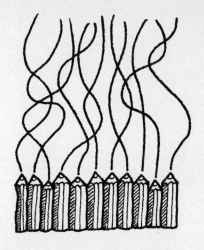

Teacher
entries

The Curious Chorus of Creation

(Based on Genesis 1:1–2:3)

Flash.
Ding-a-ling, zzzzz.
(Day 1. God created light; day and night)

Whizz, swish, whoosh.
(Day 2. God created the heavens and space)

Rumble, crunch,
Drip, plop, ripple.
Rustle, creak,
Yum, yum.
(Day 3. God created the land and sea; grass, trees and fruit)

Twinkle, twinkle.
Sparkle, sparkle.
(Day 4. God created the sun, moon and stars)

Splash, splosh,
Gurgle, gurgle.
Tweet, chirp,
Flutter, flap.
(Day 5. God created the sea creatures and the birds).

Woof, meow, squeak;
Oink, moo, baa;
Roar, growl, hiss.
Hello, hello.

Wow!
(Day 6. God created the animals – domestic and wild.
God created man and woman, Adam and Eve.
God saw everything he had made and it was very good.)

Yawn…
(Day 7. God rested from all his work.)

Jez Smith
Alderman Richard Hallam Primary School, Leicester

Jesus slept in a cardboard box

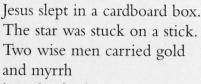

Jesus slept in a cardboard box.
The star was stuck on a stick.
Two wise men carried gold
and myrrh
'cos the frankincense king was off sick.

The shepherds all wore teatowels,
with stripes and checks and cats.
And Joseph stood in the corner
slowly unplaiting her plaits.

Three sheep with blackened noses
sat sucking their cloven feet,
while Mary wrestled with yards of cloth
as she perched on her plastic seat.

A troupe of tinselled angels
stood huddled in the wings,
where quietly flapping teachers
tied granny knots in strings.

The church filled up with parents,
and eyes filled up with tears.
Some shook with silent laughter;
with pride, with hopes and fears.

"Fear not!" squeaked Angel Gabriel,
"I bring good news today!"
And a hush fell over the stable
when our class did The Play.

Glenys Adams
St. John's CE Primary School, Waterloo, Liverpool

A current issue of love

Love is like electricity.
Powerful and productive.

Jez Smith
Alderman Richard Hallam Primary School, Leicester

The price of love

Love is free,
so share it.

Jez Smith
Alderman Richard Hallam Primary School, Leicester

The Church

Is the Church a building
made of brick or stone?
Tiny village chapel
or grand cathedral dome?
No – the Church is more than this.
It's built of people bricks,
each one very different
to provide the proper mix
of willing feet
and helpful hands.
Someone just "to be there",
someone who understands.
The tongue is very small
but it has a vital role.
Without these small important bits
the body is not whole.
The leg is as important
as the very smallest bone.
Each one has a special place;
not one should be alone.
The orchestra will be in tune
when each one plays their part.
The Church is just a building
unless it has a heart.

Carol Holman
The Abbey School, Farnham, Surrey